This special book belongs to:

_____

It is time to wake up for school, but when I open my eyes, everything looks fuzzy.

It is hard to see Mommy cooking my favorite breakfast. She's fuzzy.

I can't see the picture book my teacher is reading.
It's fuzzy.

It is lunch time, but I can't see the cafeteria sign. It's so fuzzy.

Time for recess, and I can't wait to play! Where are my friends? They're all fuzzy.

Ring! It's time to go home.
Big trucks are passing by,
but I can't see the words.
They're too fuzzy.

It is time for bed. "Mommy, sometimes I can't see so well. Things look fuzzy." Mommy says she knows exactly what to do!

Mommy takes me to a special eye doctor called an optometrist. A nice lady asks if I'd like to play a game. I do! I look into big binoculars to find the red balloon. That was fun! Then a machine blows a little puff of air into my eyes. It tickles.

The doctor shows me letters on the wall and asks me if I can see them. I can't see all of them. Still fuzzy.

He says glasses will make everything clear!

Mommy helps me try on all kinds of glasses. **Big** ones. Small ones. Brown ones. Green ones. Plastic ones. Metal ones. Round ones. Oval ones. The green ones are my favorite!

I have to wait a few days until my glasses arrive. Fuzzy eyes every day until…

the glasses-made especially for me-are ready!

Ah, no more fuzzy eyes!

About the Author

Ryan Grafenreed is a five year old kindergartener who lives outside of Atlanta, Georgia. Ryan loves reading, telling stories, playing musical instruments, traveling, karate and swimming. He is currently working on his next book, so be sure to look out for more adventures from Ryan's World!

Thank you for your support!

@ryansworld12

@ryansworld1222

RyansWorld1222@gmail.com

www.ingramcontent.com/pod-product-compliance
Lightning Source LLC
Chambersburg PA
CBHW042145290426
44110CB00002B/115